Other Titles by Joe Cacciotti

Hurricane Cores the Big Apple
Hurricane Rocks Wisconsin
Poems For The Heart
Blue Collar Real Estate Mogul "Literary Work"

Coming Soon

Hurricane Strips Las Vegas
Hurricane Strikes Rhode Island
Hurricane Mashes Idaho
Hurricane Gold Rushes California
Hurricane Volunteers in Tennessee

Poems for the Heart
Volume II

Joseph J. Cacciotti

LAURUS BOOKS

Poems For The Heart
Volume II

By Joseph J. Cacciotti

Copyright © 2012 Joseph J. Cacciotti

All rights reserved. No part of this publication may be reproduced, stored in or introduced into a retrieval system, or transmitted, in any form, or by any means (electronic, mechanical, photocopying, recording or otherwise) without the prior written permission of the publisher. Any person who commits any unauthorized act in relation to this publication may be liable to criminal prosecution and civil claims for damages.

All characters and events in this book are completely fictional and a product of the author's own imagination.

Paperback: ISBN: 978-1-938526-00-8

E-Book: ISBN: 978-1-938526-01-5

This book is sold subject to the condition that it shall not, by way of trade or otherwise, be lent, re-sold, hired out, or otherwise circulated without the publisher's prior consent in any form of binding or cover other than that in which it is published and without a similar condition including this condition being imposed on the subsequent purchaser.

Edited and designed by Nancy E. Williams
Cover by Jennifer Tipton Cappoen and Nancy E. Williams

Published by:

Laurus Books
P.O. Box 894
Locust Grove, Georgia 30248 USA
www.TheLaurusCompany.com

This book may be purchased from LaurusBooks.com, Amazon.com, and other retailers around the world.

To Diane, with love.

Contents

BEING ALONE 9
    Lonely 10
    Tell Me Why 11
    Hoping 12
    A Night To Remember 13
    I Should Have Told You 14
    Have You Seen Her 16
    Those Special Feelings 18
    You Were Mine 20
    Where Can You Be Now? 21
    I Never Told You 22
    Chance 23
    Dark Clouds 24
    If Time Heals All Wounds 25
    Tan Line 26
    Be Yourself 28

LOSING SOMEONE 29
    You Left Us Love 30
    I'm Going To Miss You 31
    Departure Of A Best Friend 33
    You're Still Here 35
    Yesterday, Today, and Tomorrow 37
    Remember 38
    Last Kiss 40
    Never To Forget 42
    Together Again 43
    Pictures 44
    Only You 46

Contents

BEAUTIFUL PEOPLE 47
- You're Special 48
- Inside Out 50
- Inner Beauty 51
- Feeling of Love 52
- At First Sight 53
- Because of You 55
- Baby, I Love You 57
- Life's Too Short 58
- After Tomorrow 59
- Happiness 61
- She Understands Me 62
- Memories 63
- Beautiful Eyes 64

LASTING WORDS 65
- We Are Americans 66
- Time Passes By 68
- Wake Up Call 70
- Precious And Few 71
- The Worst That Could Happen 72
- Worse Things Than Dying 74
- Life's Too Short 76
- Precious Time 77
- What Did They Do To You? 79
- Nothing Granted 80
- True Success 81
- No Second Chance 82

BEING ALONE

We all have felt the sting of being alone, without anyone to hold on to for hope or inspiration. Whether we want to admit it or not, we all need someone sometime. I know this because I have been there, and I know the emptiness of BEING ALONE.

I encourage finding your own personal creativity. Writing is therapeutic. I have included a few of my poems in this presentation to, hopefully, inspire you never to give up.

I believe there is someone out there for everybody.

One only needs the patience to

keep on looking ... and never give up.

—Joe

LONELY

Sitting here on the step

The night is dark and cold.

Frost telling me to go inside

But I can't.

There is no one I know

No money I own

I am lonely.

TELL ME WHY

Tell me why we have to grow older

And why time goes by so fast.

Tell me why some days grow bolder

And why everything good doesn't last.

Please tell me why.

Or maybe

You can't.

HOPING

I'm sitting here alone, like always.

And like always

Reminiscing the past

When I was not alone

I was happy

I have so many memories

Locked up inside of me

And these memories

Are the only thing

That keeps me going

Cause maybe someday

They will return.

A NIGHT TO REMEMBER

As you lit the candle on the table,
I watched the glowing light
Bounce off your face.
It was the loveliest sight
I had seen in such a long time.

Your brown eyes were glowing
Like the stars in the sky.
Your hair, so beautiful and curly, sparkled.
And when you smiled,
It hit me in such a strange way.

A way in which it felt like
Butterflies were fluttering inside my stomach.
For some reason, my heart
Felt like a magnet,
And your smile was drawing me to you.

I realized how very lucky I was
To have you by my side.
Today, I can't stop thinking about you
Because the angel I took out last night
Is the angel in my heart tonight.

I SHOULD HAVE TOLD YOU

Every time I tried to tell you,
The words would never come out.
Even though you knew how I felt,
I knew you were waiting to hear me say
Those words I should have told you.

I took it for granted you would always be here,
So I never gave it much thought.
Now I regret not saying
What I should have told you
From the start.

Yesterday you were always there
Through thick and thin.
No matter what problems we had,
Somehow we'd always work them out.
I should have told you then.

I should have told you,
What you wanted to hear.
Maybe you would still be with me.
Now, I'll drink my sorrows away,
Wishing I could begin again.

Today, you struck my heart
As I watched you walk down the aisle with him.
My heart broke in two as I heard
Your words ... I do,
Not really knowing how I felt about you.

My eyes filled up with tears.
You thought they were tears of joy.
I knew I'd just lost my best friend,
And I lost you because of three little words ...
I should have told you.

HAVE YOU SEEN HER?

Yesterday, I passed this girl on the street.
Her curly brown hair was blowing in the wind.
I was mesmerized by her graceful walk
And the way she moved her hips.
Have you seen her?

I was too timid to walk up and talk to her,
But lately she's always on my mind.
I need to find this girl
With that cute little smile.
Have you seen her?

Hey, mister, have you seen her?
She stands about five foot two,
With curly brown hair
And brown eyes, too,
With a smile that could brighten up my cloudy days.

Why didn't I stop and talk to her
When I had the chance?
Now, I'm walking the streets looking for her.
Please tell me, have you seen her?

Maybe she was just a mirage
In my mind, and she didn't exist.
I can still see her curly brown hair blowing in the wind
And the tender way she smiled at me.
Have you seen her?

I'm going to keep walking these streets
Until I find that girl who twisted my heart in a knot.
If you see me on your block,
Don't be surprised if I ask you,
Have you seen her?

Curly brown hair,
Eyes of brown,
A cute little smile.

THOSE SPECIAL FEELINGS

I was driving down the road
When a song came on the radio.
It was a song I haven't heard
In a very long time.

The words took me back to
Another place and time
When I was young
And she was mine.

This was our song
Back then, and it had
So very little meaning
We just liked the song.

Today, I can't help thinking
Thinking about the love
The love we used to share
Every time that song came on the radio.

Isn't it strange that a song
That played way back then
Could cause so many feelings
Today in my heart?

Why is it now
That when I hear that song,
My eyes tear up
Thinking of yesteryear.

I'm happy being with my family.
I have a loving wife
And three darling daughters,
Even though they are all grown up now.

Is it that the older we get
The more we tend to worship
What we had back then and
What we have now.

For whenever I hear
Certain songs from the past,
It's like my heart reminds me of
All those special feelings.

YOU WERE MINE

I was paging through my yearbook yesterday,
I saw a picture of another place and time.
And my mind starting reeling
About the time when you were mine.

Every now and then my mind drifts back,
And my face seems to shine.
So many fun times we had back then
When I was yours and you were mine.

Three whole years we were together.
You were my favorite valentine.
Even though we are far apart now,
I'll never forget when you were mine.

Time slips by, as the wise men say
And when I hear that old church bell chime
I wonder if you ever think of those days
When I was yours and you were mine

WHERE CAN YOU BE NOW?

As I was working in the basement,
I heard a song on the radio.
And my mind seemed to drift back
To a time when
I loved someone else.

Even though I'm happy now,
I couldn't help thinking about
What life could have been like
If we would have stayed together.

Every time we see a movie or watch television,
I think about you and wonder
If your dream about being a movie star
Ever came true?

It seems strange when I hear certain songs
I get goose bumps and think of you.
There are times I'd like to see you one more time
Just to find out how you're doing.

With so many memories bottled up inside
It boggles my mind, and I wonder about you.
Why? I don't really know.
   Then I ponder the question:
Where can you be now?

I NEVER TOLD YOU

I remember how I felt
When you moved in next door.
With your cute freckled face and button nose,
I knew in an instant it was you I adored.

I remember walking to school carrying your books.
You must have had a magic spell.
When you put your soft warm hand in mine,
I felt like a king, I wanted to yell.

We had so much fun.
I thought they'd never end.
Then our high school days were through.
I still never told you.

College days came in, and
We went our own way.
Even thought we are apart,
I can feel your soft sweet touch deep in my heart.

Today, my mind drifts back to those times,
And I remember how much we cared for each other.
I wonder if we'd still be together now
If I had told you how I felt

I didn't want to hold you back
From all your plans and dreams.
Because of fear I never told you.
But I dream what might have been.

CHANCE

Emptiness is all around
Around because I never
Never took a chance
Chance to ask her out
Out because I loved
Loved her from afar
Afar because I was scared
Scared about what she would say
Say because the answer
Answer could be no.

So I just watched
Watched her from a distance
A distance too far to reach
Reach and hold her tight.

Now I just sit here
Here in this room and dream
Dream about what could have been
Been if I'd only taken a chance.

DARK CLOUDS

Dark clouds cover the blue sky,
And the air is getting cold.
Just like my heart
Ever since you said good-bye.

You were the piece of the puzzle
That held our love together.
I felt like king of the world
When you were standing by my side.

I stand here now
Waiting for you to come home.
With a broken heart,
I need your love to piece it together.

My life is now empty without you.
I sit here looking out the window,
Hoping I'll see your pretty smile soon.
Please, hurry home.

IF TIME HEALS ALL WOUNDS

If time heals all wounds
Like the experts say
Why does it still hurt?
Two years after you went away?

Even today I find myself
Thinking about you everyday
Why is it everyplace I go?
I can still hear every word you say?

Some days I can't fight the tears
As they travel from my eye
Even though I say it's watering
We all know that's a lie

I find myself thinking about you
Every time I hear your favorite song
Whoever said time heals all wounds
I think they are wrong

Because whenever I feel depressed
I go to our favorite place and as I walk through
I find my wounds haven't healed
Because I still love you

TAN LINE

I was walking down the street
In the blazing summer heat
When this girl walked by.
I noticed her long sun-tanned legs
Disappearing under her high cut shorts.
I wondered where her tan line goes.

Where was she headed to?
I was enjoying the show.
I locked onto her slow motion like the ocean.
I knew it was wrong, but I just had to know
Where that tan line goes.

She had one of the sexiest walks I ever saw.
I was hypnotized by the sway of her hips
And her soft sweet smile.
My heart was doing flips as I wondered
Where her tan line goes?

Before I knew it we were standing on the beach.
I watched as she peeled out of her shorts,
Showing off the skimpiest swimsuit I'd ever seen.
I felt like I was watching the Olympic sports.
I thought I was finally going to see
Where her tan line goes.

Just as she unfastened her halter top,
I woke up and discovered it was a dream.
My dream was shattered once again.
I wanted to scream.
I never found out where her tan line goes.

BE YOURSELF

How many times can my heart be broken
Before it's beyond repair?
Everyday I search for you,
And everyday my heart feels empty.

Every time I find someone I like
They leave me for another.
What is it, I say, that makes them go away?
I wish I knew why they always leave.

Everyone says I'm kind and generous.
But if this is true, why can't I find someone
Who could fall in love with me, too,
Instead of leaving me feeling so blue.

What is it that makes me go out and look for you?
They say there's someone for everyone.
Just waiting to be kissed.
But all I need is one true love, this is my only wish.

Then again why would I want to look
When I know it will end up the same way again?
How many more times before I learn for myself
That true love can't be borrowed or bought.

Maybe if I stop trying so hard and just be myself
I will find a love that's true.
Then I might finally find a way
To truly mend this broken heart.

LOSING SOMEONE

This was a difficult chapter

for me to write.

Over the last two years, not only did

I lose my Father,

but I have lost

several wonderful friends.

It was a privilege to know them.

This is my special tribute

to honor those

who have made a difference

in my life.

YOU LEFT US LOVE

Dad, you once told me you were upset
Because you had nothing to leave us kids.
But you gave us the greatest gift anyone could ask for.
You gave us Love.

Looking down at us, you have to feel great,
Look at how many people's lives you have touched.
Your love for life and people knew no boundaries.
This is what you taught me growing up.

I just hope I can be half the man you were
And can carry that same torch of love you had for us.
You may have come into this world with nothing,
But you leave it a very wealthy man.

Wealth is not only in silver and gold
Or what you have to show.
It is what you leave behind.
Just look around this room and know.

Because of your compassion for people
And your love and understanding,
You have filled this room not with only friends,
Co-workers, relatives, and family, but with Love.

As you look down upon us now,
Even though Mom's kicking your butt
Because you put your garage over her rose garden.
I hope you feel great because of the Love you left behind.

I'M GOING TO MISS YOU

Dad, you found peace at last.
No more hurting or suffering.
Even though I'm going to miss you,
I can't be selfish and see you continue to suffer.

I'm going to miss your warm smile
And your gentle laugh.
I'm going to miss the conversations we used to have
And your understanding ways.

I'm going to miss you saying,
"Take this money, or I'll kick your ass."
Dad, I could never repay you for what you gave to me.
Every time I called, you were there for me.

Even though I've tried to repay you in certain ways
I could never even come close to closing the gap.
I'm going to miss your bear hugs
Whenever I would leave your house.

I'm going to miss the bread and butter
On Saturday mornings at your house.
I'm going to miss our Sunday morning drives
When the Packers weren't playing.

more ...

I'm going to miss those Sunday evenings
Yelling and screaming at the Packer games.
Most of all, Dad, I'm going to miss your phone calls
And spending time with you.

I'm going to miss your patented moon walks
And your cute little chuckle.
I'm going to miss your sense of humor
And how nothing ever seemed to bother you.

Most of all, when a tear flows down my cheek,
It's not that I'm crying for you.
I'm crying for me and the thought
What I'll be missing when I think of you.

Now you've found the peace you deserve.
I know someday we'll be together once again.
But until that time rolls around, let me just say
I'm going to miss you, Dad.

DEPARTURE OF A BEST FRIEND

He was loyal and true
All the way to the end.
Gary T. was a husband, a father,
And most of all, he was
One of my best friends.

Thirty-two years ago, we first met.
We didn't know each other that well.
I played so many jokes on him,
But he never became upset.

I had a hard time at first
When I heard he had died.
I'm not too proud to say
I went down on my knees and cried.

He was the kind of person,
He'd give you the shirt off of his back.
Friendship and kindness
Are the two things he never lacked.

more ...

Going to baseball games, long drives
Or just sitting at the seven-mile fair.
We'd always have fun playing cribbage,
And you could tell how much he cared.

Now I must say farewell to my friend
But this isn't really the end.
I know, sooner or later, buddy,
We'll meet up again.

YOU'RE STILL HERE

I close my eyes and listen
To the music that once was ours.
My heart grows warm inside,
And I realize you're still here with me.

I still feel your soft touch
When you take my hand in yours
As we slowly walk
Out to dance in the living room.

Some experts say that time heals all wounds,
But my heart seems to grow stronger for you
With every passing year—
I just can't let you go.

It took me a long time
To find a woman like you.
You were so alive and energetic,
Always on the go.

We had so much fun
In the ten short years we were together,
Before we found out you were sick,
And my love for you grew stronger

more ...

It hurt me that I couldn't help.
I watched you wither away
Right down to your bones.
Cancer took you away from me.

But tonight I can feel you in my arms
Dancing with me once again.
I know you're still here—
I can feel you in my heart.

YESTERDAY, TODAY, AND TOMORROW

Yesterday the sun was warm,
And my heart was full of happiness.
You were here next to me,
Walking hand in hand through the park.
We were on a wonderful ride
That I thought would never end.

Why did we have to be out
On the road that night?
Even though my thermometer reads 90
I feel so cold inside.
We never saw that drunken driver
Until it was too late.

Today, I can feel you,
I can feel your soft skin.
As I hold you against my body,
I can feel your heart beat against mine,
As once again we're together.

Then my alarm clock wakes me up,
And I discover it was all a dream,
A dream I hold deep inside my heart.
My eyes fill up with tears
As I come back to reality
Realizing once again that you are gone.

REMEMBER

It seems like yesterday
On that rainy night
You turned to me and asked,
"Will you remember me?"

There are so many ways
I'll remember you.
You gave me love and comfort
On those tough, trying days.

You were there
When I needed you most,
Especially when my
Mother passed away.

You were my strength
When I felt tired and weak.
When I had to climb that mountain,
You were there to hold my hand.

I had all the riches
I could ever have needed
When you became part of my life.
After 29 years, the fire is still there.

I remember you for the kindness
You gave not only to me
But countless others, no matter
If they were friend or foe.

I remember you for making me a better man
And how to see things from a different view.
Through rich times and poor,
You stayed by my side.

I remember how tough you were
And how I cried
When I sat by your side
Holding your hand when you died.

LAST KISS

I sit here inside this room
Thinking about the times we once shared
You danced so close to me
I could feel your heart beat.

Some of our friends
Said we made the perfect couple
We never had to say anything
We could read each other's mind.

I remember how beautiful you looked
In that white dress
And your lovely smile
That stuck to your face that whole night

I was on cloud nine
Knowing you were mine forever.
We sang love songs all the way
To our special room.

We never saw that truck lose control
Until it was to late
I remember hearing our screams
And the sound of busting glass.

Somehow I found you
Even though I had blood blocking my vision.
As I held you in my arms
You smiled and whispered, kiss me.

I felt your trembling lips against mine.
The beating of your heart slowed.
I kissed you one last time and held you.
Your body turned cold slowly in my arms.

Now, I sit inside these walls,
These four walls that now are so silent.
Slowly a tear streams down my face
I'll never forget our last kiss.

NEVER TO FORGET

It's been a year already since you passed away, Dad.
You once told me that time heals all wounds.
But it never patches up the emptiness it leaves behind.
You wanted your remembrance to be a happy one.
Only problem is, Dad, you never left us any sad moments.
You were always upbeat and always thinking in a positive way,
And you never, ever turned your back on your fellow man.
You never had a bad thing to say about anyone, or anything.
You always tried to keep the family close knit.
Not just the siblings, but Aunts, Uncles and Cousins as well.
You even instilled in me something that I'll always treasure,
And that is to treat people as I want to be treated.
It never mattered what color, creed, or religion they were.
Because of that, I never have or ever will judge a person by the
Color of their skin or their beliefs.
Dad, these tears I cry now are because I miss you.
You were the glue that held our family together,
And now we seem so distant.
Dad, maybe in time they will also see that bright candle
You bestowed upon everyone when you were around.
After all, you gave everyone the greatest gift of all—
Love.

TOGETHER AGAIN

Sometimes life throws you a curve ball
And no matter what you do, nothing helps.
Today, even though the sky is blue,
My mind is full of clouds.

I can't seem to think straight.
My mind wanders to a different place and time.
Everywhere I go and everything thing I see
Brings back memories of you

When I look into a window,
I can see you looking back at me.
When I fall asleep, I can feel you next to me.
I feel your soft sweet touch.

But every morning when I wake up,
I'm still very much alone.
I can still feel my love for you,
Even though now you're in a different place.

Time, they say, heals all wounds.
But it doesn't mend a broken heart.
However, I know we will meet up again someday.
And when that day comes, we'll be together again.

PICTURES

I used to make fun of my father
Every time he would
Bring out his camera.
He would walk around
Taking pictures of everyone.

I realize now that he is gone
Why taking pictures are so important.
I remember my father in spirit,
But I wish I had more pictures
To help me remember those happy moments.

Because once your loved ones are gone,
The only thing you have left
Are your fun-filled memories.
But a picture can help mend
Your broken heart.

I remember back when I was young
And the fun we once had
Together as a family.
I can still relive those days
Looking at these pictures.

What really takes my breath away
Is when I'm looking at these pictures.
It feels like my mother and father
Are still standing by my side
Looking at them with me.

Just think, I used to laugh at my father
When he took all of these pictures.
Now, I cry every time I look at them.
I wish he had taken many more.

ONLY YOU

Today, my mind is cloudy
Cloudy because of the memories
Memories of when we were together
Together and full of happiness
Happiness and I felt so alive
Alive because we were in love
In love and full of life
A life that was suddenly changed
Changed because you were taken
Taken away quietly while you were sleeping
Sleeping without warning or pain
Pain is now what I feel deep in my heart
Heart that is now empty
Empty except for the memories
Memories of when we were together
Together, always, and forever
Forever because I know
I know our love was true
True because you are the only one
Only one I've ever loved
Loved because there was only one
One person whom I've loved my whole life
Life that will never be the same again
Again because there was only one love for me
For me there was Only You.

BEAUTIFUL PEOPLE

Have you ever noticed all the beautiful people

in this world who are teased so much about their

appearances that they suffer emotional scars and

tend to believe they would be better off ending their

lives? I have combined a few poems for those special

people, along with a few of my newest Love poems.

I'd like to express a sincere thank you

to three very special people—

Sierra Braun,

Estreya Vasquez,

and Vinni Ricchio

—for giving me the inspiration

for a few of my poems.

Inspiration for this poem is
because of my good friend Sierra Braun

YOU'RE SPECIAL

I saw a girl in the corner with
Tears rolling down from her eyes.
Trying to be helpful
I went over and asked her, Why?

She said kids were picking on her
Because of the freckles on her face.
I said those are special freckles
That shows your elegance and grace.

She looked up and asked,
Why are kids so cruel?
I said because some kids forgot
One of God's most important rules.

Don't do unto others
As they would do to you.
He's made everyone special.
This much I know is true.

You are very special,
Unique in every way.
I bet your smile with all your freckles
Brightens up other people's days.

Someday you'll look back and discover
That what I say is true
Because, when I went to school,
I was picked on, too.

She looked at me, a smile from ear to ear.
It touched my heart in the warmest way.
Now I know why God gave you freckles—
You're beautiful, my dear.

INSIDE OUT

Why do you make fun
Of that person in the corner
When you don't even know her?

Just because you didn't have to raise
Three kids on your own,
Doesn't make you any better.

Look at those kids gathered all around her.
Even though she looks tired,
She still laughs and has a smile on her face.

She may not have a lot of money.
Still she is richer than you and me.
She has love written all over her face.

You can see her kids laughing
And playing together with her.
That kind of love can't be bought or sold.

You might laugh at her looks on the outside
But what stands out more to me
Is how beautiful she really is from the inside out.

INNER BEAUTY

Have you ever looked
into someone's soul
and seem the inner beauty
they possess?

Looked past the warm smile
and cute button nose,
the smooth tender skin,
and the tight-fitting clothes?

You have to dig deep
and play it smart,
just find out first
what's inside their heart.

What is outside the body
is easy to see,
but it's what on the inside
that will make you believe.

Beauty starts on the inside,
down deep in the soul,
and when it filters out, that's
when it makes your heart glow.

So don't make fun
of what you can't see.
Beauty is in the eye of the beholder
and she belongs to me.

These next three poems were inspired by
Estreya Vasquez and Vinni Ricchio.

FEELING OF LOVE

I can feel your heartbeat
Even when you're far away.
I wonder if you can feel mine, too,
And know how happy I am with you.

My life seemed empty
Until I held you in my arms
And felt the warm tenderness
In your kiss.

I know our love has no bounds.
It seems our lives are now complete.
It's as if we were always
Meant to be together.

When I look into your beautiful brown eyes.
You don't even have to talk
Because I can see how much
You love me, too.

Just thinking about you
Lying here in bed,
My life is full of happiness and love.
I can feel your heartbeat.

AT FIRST SIGHT

When I first saw you,
You took my breath away.
I couldn't speak,
You took my breath away.

With your soft beautiful smile,
You looked like an angel.
As the sunshine reflected off your face,
I saw a glow from up above.

Even before we ever met,
I knew deep down inside
You were the one for me.
All I had to do was tell you.

But every time I had my chance,
I froze not knowing what to say.
Instead, we became friends.
Everyday we spent together warmed my heart.

Suddenly, my heart started telling me something.
I felt myself always wanting to be with you.
Then on that magical night as we were bowling,
I couldn't hold back any longer.

more ...

When I asked you to go steady,
I saw the glow in your eyes.
Then your beautiful smile invaded my mind.
My heart exploded as your lips met mine.

Honey, you bring out the best in me.
I never knew I could feel like this.
Even though it took me a while to ask,
Some things are definitely worth the wait.

BECAUSE OF YOU

It started back in seventh grade
When our eyes first met.
You looked so cute.
Even though we didn't know each other.
I had a hard time listening to the teacher
Because of you.

I remember running home that day
Telling my mom about this cute Mexican boy I saw.
It didn't even matter to me
When I was told you were Italian.
I had a hard time sleeping that night
Because of you.

When you finally said hello to me,
I thought I'd faint. When I heard your sweet voice,
I became tongue-tied and almost couldn't speak.
My heart was pounding so hard
I thought everyone around heard it
Because of you.

Later in our lives, you asked me for a date.
You took me moonlight bowling.
We were having so much fun
I was having a hard time
Concentrating on the game
Because of you

more ...

Suddenly, you looked at me
And asked me to be your girl.
I thought I was dreaming.
I asked you to repeat the question.
Then our lips finally met, and my heart was warm
Because of you.

My life is now complete
And happiness is all around.
You're the sunlight in my life.
And when you hold me in your arms,
It feels like our hearts are connected
Because of you.

*This poem was inspired by two of my good friends,
Estreya Vasquez and Vinni Ricchio.*

BABY, I LOVE YOU

Today, when I woke up,
I couldn't help thinking about you.
I thought about how beautiful
You looked last night.

Every time I remember your sweet little laugh,
I feel warm deep in my heart.
I can still feel your soft fingers perfectly
Wrapping around mine like a warm glove.

I remember when we kissed
How soft and passionate it felt.
Even though we are apart now,
I can still feel the butterflies inside my stomach.

Tonight, when we are together again,
And I am holding you close,
I will not be able to refrain from
Telling you how I feel—
 Baby, I love you.

LIFE'S TOO SHORT

Life is too short,
My father would always say.
Don't worry about tomorrow.
Just live for today.

I never understood those words
Until the day he passed away.
Never get upset or angry because
You never know when it could be your last day.

All those times I should have told him how I felt
But never thought it was important.
I'd like to go back to those days and tell him
How I feel now, but I can't.

Today, there isn't a day that goes by
When I don't tell people how I feel.
So when you say something to someone,
Make sure it's sincere and real.

Because when your number is up,
There's nothing you can do.
But if you leave this world with love,
People will always remember you.

AFTER TOMORROW

What is it about you
That intrigues me so?
Is it your cute freckled face,
Your button nose, or your
Lovely bright smile
That warms my heart?

Since the day we met,
All I have had on my mind
Is you.
I've been around many girls before,
But no one has captured my heart
The way you do.

Whenever we are together,
I feel so complete inside.
And when we are apart,
I have this empty feeling
Inside my heart.

I wonder if you realize
What you do to me.
Every time you're near me,
I want to wrap you up in my arms
And never let you go.

more ...

When I feel your soft tender lips
Kissing mine from the start
I wonder if you feel the fireworks
Shooting through my heart.

Tonight, my friends are envious.
They tell me I'm a lucky man.
Tomorrow, when I see you walking
Down the aisle, I'll know they are right
Because I know forever you will be mine.

HAPPINESS

With you by my side,
I can conquer the world.
My life is full
Of happiness and hope.

Together, we can build
Strong family ties
And show others
What true love is about.

My love for you
Knows no bounds.
You've changed me
Into the man I am today.

I can only pray others
Could feel the way I do
Because, if they could, maybe
This world would be a beautiful place
Once again.

SHE UNDERSTANDS ME

Who sent you here?
I never thought I'd ever meet someone like you.
No matter what I do or say,
She understands me.

Even though I try to do things right,
When I grow impatient and want to stop,
She hugs me tight and whispers into my ear.
I settle down and melt into her arms.

What is this magic every time she's around?
Nothing seems impossible when she is near.
I feel relaxed and motivated.
She understands me.

When she is near, I get all tongue-tied.
Even though no words come out,
She knows exactly what I'm going to say.
Then she brushes her soft lips up to mine.

She knows when I am troubled
As she takes my hand in hers.
Our fingers fold together like a glove.
Truly she understands me.

MEMORIES

I noticed you
When you walked into the room.
For some strange reason,
I couldn't take my eyes off of you.

I watched as you gracefully
Walked across the room.
Your hips swayed with a motion
So seductive with each step.

Your face had a warm glow.
Every time you smiled,
I found myself smiling with you
Even though we were apart.

I was a little speechless at first
When you said hello.
Then you reached out to take my hand,
And it was like we were old friends.

We laughed and talked
The whole night through.
Now, as I think back, my life is complete.
It all started the day I noticed you.

BEAUTIFUL EYES

Why do you hide your beautiful eyes
Behind those dark sunglasses?
I realize the sun is bright,
But that just enhances your colorful gaze.

You're cat-like eyes should be displayed
Every minute of the day.
Your eyes can tell a lot about you,
Whether you're happy or mad, silly or sad.

So please take off those dark glasses.
I want to look at those beautiful eyes
And see the real person you are deep down inside.
Maybe you'll touch my heart because what they say is true.

Beauty is only skin deep.
Your sexy body is just a cover up
For what is really deep down inside.
If you really want to show how gorgeous you are.

Let them look into your beautiful eyes,
So they can see the real person you are.
Tight pants and halter tops can turn some heads,
But beautiful eyes can stop them in their tracks.

So don't hide behind those dark glasses
Show the world, the real you.
And show those beautiful eyes
Every chance you get.

LASTING WORDS

After my father passed away,

I started thinking about

things he used to tell me

when he was alive.

I have included

some of his words

into these next few poems,

so you can see that

what he was telling me

was true.

WE ARE AMERICANS

What's wrong with this country of ours?
We preach for ending the violence in Iraq.
Are we so blind we can't see the violence
In our own backyard?

"United we stand"
At one time meant something.
We cared, no matter how much money
A person has, or what he owns.

We have to get over
Our personal greed for money.
We have to bring back our spirit
To help each other in need.

Why do we help only during tragedy?
Remember 911 and the way
Thousands of people came to help
In that time of need?

Where are all those people now?
Why can't we live every day as we did
When our brothers and sisters
Died that fateful day?

*What happened to those people?
If we can come together in times of tragedy
And at Christmas, then why not
Come together every other day of the year?

Americans are supposed to be united,
Not fighting against one another.
Everyone has their own point of view
Nobody is entirely right or wrong.

This is the land of the free
And the home of the brave,
Not bullies and thugs
As we are today.

We are supposed to be better
Than other nations
Of the world.
WE ARE AMERICANS.*

TIME PASSES BY

I'm looking into my bedroom mirror
And wondering where that old man came from.
It seems like only yesterday
I had muscles where now there are none.

Now all my muscles have turned to flab
And settled around my midsection.
I can't bend over and touch my toes,
Or the button on my pants will blow.

The pitty patter of little feet running
Down our hallway always made me smile.
Those little girls are all grown up
Now with families of their own.

My energy level was always on go
But somehow it got up and left.
The boy who worked hard rebuilding houses
Now wears on bad knees and shoulders pain patches.

I remember when I told my father
That I couldn't wait to grow up.
Don't wish your life away, he said,
It will fly right on by soon enough.

Now I'm past fifty and wishing
I could go back to being young again.
When little feet ran these lonesome halls
And my wife said I looked like a hunk.

If I could go back in time
With the knowledge I have today,
I'd probably do the same things I've done
But in a little different way.

However, if I did get another chance,
Would I have what I have now?
A loving wife, three darling daughters,
And a heart full of wonderful memories.

Time passes on
And all I can say
Is thank you for the lovely memories
I still have of yesterday.

WAKE UP CALL

Today, I saw a bright orange glow
Slowly creeping higher and higher
It looked like the clouds were on fire
As another new day arose.

The sun glistened upon the calm water
As if it were admiring itself
Looking into the mirrored lake
A breathtaking view, spectacular.

Everyone asks me why I wake up
So early in the morning.
It's so I can witness once more the splendor
Of the easterly sun slowly rising.

And for an extra added bonus
It washes, at day's end, the western sky
With radiant and restful colors
When the sun helps prepare us for night.

This is why I often say,
Until you witness it for yourself,
You'll never understand why this is
Certainly the best part of the day.

PRECIOUS AND FEW

I had a dream the other night,
A dream that everyone
Lived together
In peace and harmony.

There were no more
Bigotry or racial slurs.
Everyone lived and laughed
Together like one big family.

It was a world in which
Everyone treated everybody
With respect and kindness
The way it is supposed to be.

After all, we are all immigrants
In this big world,
But as we live here together
We are Americans.

Last night I had a dream
About one great man.
He tried his best in his time
To live together in peace.

I still remember those
Four words he once said
That will live in us forever …
I have a dream.

THE WORST THAT COULD HAPPEN

When I was younger, I had no idea what life was about,
I was always worried about what could happen,
Always tempted to ask a question,
But worried it might make me look dumb.

Now I think back to what I had missed along the way.
There are no guarantees in life, only opportunities.
When you find yourself worried about asking a simple question,
Ask yourself what's the worse that could happen.

So go up and ask that cute girl to walk her home,
Or go ask that young lady to go out with you.
You just might be surprised at the answer you receive.
The worse that could happen, she says no.

But what if the answer is yes?
You start by taking walks in the park.
Later, you go out to the movies or dances.
And, along the way, you find out you can't live without her.

Butterflies in your stomach seem to come to life,
Every time you are together, and you feel great inside.
You can't help thinking about each other, when you are apart
Now you have something else on your mind.

As you watch her walk down the aisle
She has a radiant glow on her face,
With a smile so bright it lights up the church.
You feel like a king as she stands next to you.

Three year later, as you talk to your child,
You remember what your father told you back then:
Don't be afraid to ask a question because
What's the worse that could happen?

WORSE THINGS
THAN DYING

I have never had any fear about dying.
Dying would be the easy way out.
As I drive down the street,
I think of many things
That would be worse than dying.

I think about the people with Alzheimer's.
The memories they once had are gone.
I think about those who battle cancer
Everyday of their lives. Even though some survive,
Their lifestyles are changed.

I think about all the people
With Muscular Dystrophy,
And any other crippling disease,
That strips their strength
Never to live life the way it should be.

I think about our soldiers,
And the sacrifices they make to keep us free.
Many have returned with missing body parts,
Even though new limbs have replaced them,
It isn't the same as when they left.

Mostly, I think about the little kids
Who get molested and beat every single day.
It turns my stomach when I read about such events.
Why is there so much hate in our world?

I've had people tell me to go to hell,
Could hell be worse than this?
I just sit back and tell myself
There are worse things than dying.

LIFE'S TOO SHORT

You only go around once in life,
So live life to its fullest.
Never let it pull you down
Or worry what tomorrow may bring.

Life is a roller-coaster ride
With many of ups and downs,
Along with a few winding curves.
Stay strong and things will work themselves out.

If you have a troubled heart,
Please find someone to talk to.
Live your life as it is supposed to be.
Don't worry what others think.

Go out and have fun.
Enjoy the time you have upon this earth.
The greatest thing about life
Is that no two people are alike.

So go out and enjoy the time you have
Upon this planet we call earth.
For you never know when
The Lord above will call your name.

So don't worry and sweat
The little things in life.
There's nothing that can't be solved except one ...
That life's too short.

PRECIOUS TIME

I remember spending time with my friends.
We'd play baseball at the park in the summer,
And sled down the hills in the winter.
We were too young back then to know
How precious that time was.

I remember learning how to rebuild
Houses from a perfect stranger.
Later, he became one of my best friends.
I didn't realize back then how precious
That time was that we spent together.

I remember all the scouting trips
My father and I shared together
Along with all of our friends.
We stayed together for thirteen years.
Those were indeed precious times.

Today, I wonder what happened
To all those great times in my life.
Where are all my friends and family?
What happened to all that time
We spent together.

more ...

As I look into my kids' eyes,
I can't help wondering if they
Realize how great life really is.
And they can enjoy Precious Time
They spend with their friends and family.

Life is too short to worry about the little things.
Live each day like it was your last
Because you never know
When your number will be called,
And you precious time will be over.

WHAT DID THEY DO TO YOU?

There is a pain shooting through my heart
Because of these stories in the paper.
Stories about some people mistreating their children,
And it turns my stomach into knots.

Why would some people treat kids with such cruelty?
Why would you tie them up, or put them in cages?
What did these innocent children do to deserve this?
How could you treat anyone with so much hate?

Kids are supposed to be treated with tender-loving care.
They are not put on this earth to be slaves.
Someday they could be taking care of you,
So why would you want to break their spirit?

What did they do to you
To deserve this kind of punishment?
I'd like to treat those who have harmed these children
The same way they treated their kids.

I've never believed that two wrongs make a right,
But with what they put these kids through,
This should never go unpunished,
And the same thing should be done to them.

Many questions shoot through my mind
As I try to get this ugly feeling out of my mind.
I'd like to ask some of these people
What did they do to you?

NOTHING GRANTED

Don't take life for granted
Because one thing you can't control
Is when your time on earth is through,
And the Lord above takes your soul.

So live your life every day
Like it could be your last.
For it could be any moment
You could be taken fast.

Life is certainly more precious
Than anything you could buy.
So why do people treat others badly
Then laugh at them when they cry.

It doesn't matter how old you are.
Age has no boundaries, we know this is true.
So don't take life for granted, to your own self be true.
In the end, you'll have friends who truly do love you.

There is only one thing for granted.
That is truly our best reward.
That if we treat others with love,
We will be sitting next to the Lord.

TRUE SUCCESS

Look around you
Do you see all these people?
Gathered here to see you?
Don't you notice how they listen?
As you talk about your life.

Listen to them laugh
As you tell your jokes.
You have touched their hearts
In ways others wish they could.

Why do you think your life is worthless?
I wish I had the courage to do what you do,
As you stand up there and tell your life story,
Knowing full well how short your life really is.

I see the beautiful person you truly are
As you gain respect from the people listening.
Their appreciation knows no bounds.
You truly have the knack for finding the best in others.

Remember when you told me once
You wanted to be successful at something?
Take a look around you, my friend,
You have made life easier for many others.

You may not have lots of money,
You may not have fancy clothes.
But what you have is friendship and love.
This is what it's like to have Success.

NO SECOND CHANCE

All I've ever wanted to do
Since we were married
Was to try to make your life easier.
But it seemed no matter what I tried to do,
We slipped farther and farther from my goal.

There was a time when I thought I'd made it,
When you were able to stay home
And raise our children.
However, it didn't last long.
And, once again, you had to go back to work.

Even though I never said thank you,
For some reason you knew how I felt.
But deep down inside it hurt
Because I knew I had failed.
Once again, I was laid off my job.

It seems like for every step forward,
I fall two steps behind.
I wonder at times if this is what
My role in life was supposed to be.
But still I push for another tomorrow.

I've been trying so hard to find a peaceful tomorrow
That I've missed all the important yesterdays.
My children are now grown women.
I wonder how they grew so fast.
Was I really too blind to see what I missed?

Now that I'm older, I realize
I always had the riches I was looking for
And they were right under my nose.
Life isn't striving for what you don't have.
Life is how you live from day to day.

Don't worry about the things you don't have.
Enjoy the things you have before you.
Life is a journey, and you have two choices.
Go with the flow and enjoy it while it lasts,
Or take a chance and end it sooner than it starts.

There's only one sure thing in life.
There is no SECOND CHANCE.

Joseph J. Cacciotti

Joseph Cacciotti grew up in Racine, Wisconsin, along the shores of Lake Michigan. His desire to write appeared early in life when his high school teachers encouraged him to write poetry and to become a journalist. His drive to write fiction grew stronger as he matured.

Joe made a promise to his friend and mentor, Harold A. Schink, on his deathbed. Harold asked Joe to never stop writing. Joe has been faithful to that promise. In 2006, he published *Poems for the Heart*, fifty of his most talked about poems, and *Blue Collar Real Estate Mogul*, a biography based on true life experiences that he and his best friend endured as landlords in Racine and about a friendship that never stopped growing, even after death.

Joe is currently working on a series of books about "Hurricane" Samuel James Rufus, an unconventional detective whose methods for getting the bad guys come close to crossing ethical and legal lines in his pursuit of justice. Every story reveals more about the Hurricane. At times, you might ask yourself who the real bad guys are, when something more evil than the devil himself is called upon to balance off justice.

Joe lives with his wife Diane in Racine, Wisconsin. They have three daughters and a son. Joe continues to write the next books in the "Hurricane Sam Rufus" series.

www.ingramcontent.com/pod-product-compliance
Lightning Source LLC
Chambersburg PA
CBHW070856050426
42453CB00012B/2240